About This Book

Title: *Flags*

Step: 2

Word Count: 115

Skills in Focus: L-blends

Tricky Words: poles, fly, ships, blow, race, done, stripes, star

Ideas For Using This Book

Before Reading:
- **Comprehension:** Look at the title and cover image together. Walk through the pictures in the book with readers and have them make predictions about what they might learn in the book. Help them make connections by asking what they already know about flags.
- **Accuracy:** Practice saying the tricky words listed on page 1.
- **Phonemic Awareness:** Explain to readers that a blend is two consonants together that each make a sound. Discuss that some blends include the letter *L.* Read aloud story words containing L-blends, beginning with *flag*. Segment the sounds in the word slowly and have the students call out the word. Call attention to each blend and where it is found within the word.

During Reading:
- Have readers point under each word as they read it.
- **Decoding:** If readers are stuck on a word, help them say each sound and blend the sounds together smoothly. You may want to point out L-blends as they appear.
- **Comprehension:** Invite students to talk about what new things they are learning about flags while reading. What are they learning that they didn't know before?

After Reading:
Discuss the book. Some ideas for questions:
- What are flags and why do we fly them?
- Where do flags fly? What flags have you seen?
- What shapes and colors are on flags?

Flags

Text by Marley Richmond

Reading Consultant
Deborah MacPhee, PhD
Professor, School of Teaching and Learning
Illinois State University

PICTURE WINDOW BOOKS
a capstone imprint

A flag is flat. We put flags on big poles.

Flags fly in lots of spots.

Flags will flap in wind.

Flags will flip,
flop, and slap!

Flags can be still when it is calm.

Flags are still if the wind does not blow.

Flags can flap to tell you a race is done.

Kids grip flags and kids flick flags.

We put up flags.

Flags can be fun.

Black flags can flap on bad ships.

Flags can get big slits.

Flags can have flat stripes.

Stripes can be big and fat. They can be slim.

Flags can have a dot.

Flags can have a star.

Flags fly in lots of spots. Flags are fun!

More Ideas:

Phonemic Awareness Activity

Practicing L-Blends:
Tell readers they will segment the sounds of story words containing L-blends. Say an L-blend word for readers to segment the sounds. They will slowly stretch out the sounds of the word, tapping the table as they produce each sound.

Suggested words:
- flag
- help
- flap
- flick

Extended Learning Activity

Let Your Flag Fly:
Every flag looks different. Have readers think about what colors and shapes they would put on their own flags. Ask them to make drawings showing their personal flags. Ask readers about how their flags are similar to flags they have seen in this book or out in the world. How are they different? Ask readers to write a short description of their flags. Challenge them to use words with L-blends.

Published by Picture Window Books, an imprint of Capstone
1710 Roe Crest Drive, North Mankato, Minnesota 56003
capstonepub.com

Copyright © 2026 by Capstone.
All rights reserved. No part of this publication may be reproduced in whole or in part, or stored in a retrieval system, or transmitted in any form or by any means, electronic, mechanical, photocopying, recording, or otherwise, without written permission of the publisher.

Library of Congress Cataloging-in-Publication Data is available on the Library of Congress website.

ISBN: 9798875226991 (hardback)
ISBN: 9798875229732 (paperback)
ISBN: 9798875229718 (eBook PDF)

Image Credits: iStock: ezypix, 5, Orietta Gaspari, 16, simonkr, 10–11, Yau Ming Low, 6, 24; Shutterstock: Andrejs Marcenko, 17, Angirakz, 18, clearviewstock, 22–23, Dragan Mujan, 12–13, FamVeld, 14–15, GODFRY, 19, Joaquin Corbalan P, 2–3, justit, cover, Khalid Nawaz, 21, Maria Kray, 1, 7, Mick Harper, 8–9, NayaDadara, 4, Ricardorondon, 20

Printed and bound in China. PO 6274